GRADE

Success With
Writing

■ SCHOLASTIC

Editor: Ourania Papacharalambous
Cover design by Tannaz Fassihi; cover illustration by Kevin Zimmer
Interior design by Cynthia Ng
Interior illustrations by Doug Jones (8, 10, 12, 19, 30–33, 39, 41, 43);
Roger Simó (5–7, 9, 11, 15–16, 20, 22, 24–25, 27, 29, 37, 44–45)

ISBN 978-1-338-79875-3
Scholastic Inc., 557 Broadway, New York, NY 10012
Copyright © 2022 Scholastic Inc.
All rights reserved. Printed in the U.S.A.
First printing, January 2022
1 2 3 4 5 6 7 8 9 10   40   29 28 27 26 25 24 23 22

INTRODUCTION

One of the greatest challenges teachers and parents face is helping students develop independent writing skills. Each writing experience is unique and individualized. The high-interest topics and engaging exercises in *Scholastic Success With Writing* will both stimulate and encourage students as they develop their writing skills. On page 4, you will find a list of the key skills covered in this book. These grade-appropriate skills can be used in daily writing assignments such as journals, stories, and letters to help build confident, independent writers. Like a stepladder, this book will help students reach the next level of independent writing.

TABLE OF CONTENTS

Grade-Appropriate Skills Covered in Scholastic Success With Writing: Grade 5

Write opinion pieces on topics or texts, supporting a point of view with reasons and information.

Introduce a topic or text clearly, state an opinion, and create an organizational structure in which ideas are logically grouped to support the writer's purpose.

Provide logically ordered reasons that are supported by facts and details.

Link opinion and reasons using words, phrases, and clauses.

Provide a concluding statement or section related to the opinion presented.

Write informative/explanatory texts to examine a topic and convey ideas and information clearly.

Introduce a topic clearly, provide a general observation and focus, and group related information logically; include formatting (e.g., headings), illustrations, and multimedia when useful to aiding comprehension.

Develop the topic with facts, definitions, concrete details, quotations, or other information and examples related to the topic.

Link ideas within categories of information using words, phrases, and clauses.

Use precise language and domain-specific vocabulary to inform about or explain the topic.

Provide a concluding statement or section related to the information or explanation presented.

Write narratives to develop real or imagined experiences or events using effective technique, descriptive details, and clear event sequences.

Orient the reader by establishing a situation and introducing a narrator and/or characters; organize an event sequence that unfolds naturally.

Use narrative techniques, such as dialogue, description, and pacing, to develop experiences and events or show the responses of characters to situations.

Use a variety of transitional words, phrases, and clauses to manage the sequence of events.

Use concrete words and phrases and sensory details to convey experiences and events precisely.

Provide a conclusion that follows from the narrated experiences or events.

Demonstrate command of the conventions of standard English grammar and usage when writing or speaking.

Demonstrate command of the conventions of standard English capitalization, punctuation, and spelling when writing.

Use a comma to separate an introductory element from the rest of the sentence.

Use knowledge of language and its conventions when writing, speaking, reading, or listening.

Body Facts

A **sentence** is a group of words that expresses a complete thought.
There are four kinds of sentences.

A **declarative sentence** is a **statement**. It gives information and ends with a period.

I just finished a really cool article about the body.

An **interrogative sentence** is a **question**. It asks for information and often begins with *who, what, where, when, why,* or *how*. A question ends with a question mark.

What is the title of the article?

An **imperative sentence** is a **command**. It tells or asks someone to do something. A command usually ends with a period but can also end with an exclamation point.

Tell me where you read it. Hurry up and tell me!

An **exclamatory sentence** is an **exclamation**. It shows strong feeling or emotion and ends with an exclamation point.

I can't wait to read it now!

• •

**Use any or all of the words in each group to write four kinds of sentences.
One sentence has been completed for you. Begin and end each sentence correctly.**

> do how you many times breathe minute is per that count twenty humans fast

Interrogative: *How many times per minute do humans breathe?*

Declarative: _____

Imperative: _____

Exclamatory: _____

> sixty-five believe the is body water about percent I it don't really

Interrogative: _____

Declarative: _____

Imperative: _____

Exclamatory: _____

Clearly Interesting

A sentence may be very simple, but you can make it more interesting by adding **adverbs**, **adjectives**, and **prepositional phrases**. When you add to a sentence, you expand it.

The kitten ran.

adjectives   **adverb**   **prepositional phrase**

The frightened, little kitten ran quickly <u>under the bed.</u>

Add to each list of adjectives, adverbs, and prepositional phrases that has been started.

Adjectives	Adverbs	Prepositional Phrases	
lonely	calmly	over the bridge	with my friends
old	eagerly	through the woods	until noon
friendly	frequently	across the lake	during rush hour
beautiful	yesterday	out of the building	into the water

_____ _____ _____

_____ _____ _____

_____ _____ _____

_____ _____ _____

Use some of the words and phrases from above to expand each sentence.

1 The baby cried. _____

2 The man walked. _____

3 The students sat. _____

4 I went. _____

Sentence Sense

It is important to choose and arrange the words and phrases in your sentences so that what you intend to say is clear to your readers.

Eating a bowl of curds and whey, a spider frightened Miss Muffet away.

Who was eating the curds and whey, the spider or Miss Muffet? You are probably familiar with the nursery rhyme, so you know that it was Miss Muffet, but the intended meaning is not clear in the above sentence. Notice the difference in the revised sentence.

While Miss Muffet was eating a bowl of curds and whey, a spider frightened her away.

The intended meaning is unclear in the sentences below. Rearrange each sentence to make the meaning clear. As you revise, remember that you can also add and remove words. There may be more than one possible way to fix each sentence.

1 The students cheered for their team in the bleachers.

_____

2 The saleswoman sold shirts to the tourists with rainbows on them.

_____

3 As a preschooler, Dad taught me to read.

_____

4 Wading in the shallow water, just 20 feet away porpoises were swimming from us.

_____

5 While emptying the dishwasher this morning, the dog started barking at me.

_____

6 We heard about the missing painting that was found on the news today.

_____

Reread some of your recent writing. Find several sentences in which the intended meaning is not as clear as it could be. Rewrite the sentences on another sheet of paper.

Get to the Point

When you write, it is important to be clear and concise. Sometimes a sentence can have too many words or words that are not necessary. Compare the two sentences.

The audience couldn't hear what the speaker was saying on account of the fact that the microphone wasn't turned on because someone forgot.

The audience couldn't hear the speaker because the microphone wasn't turned on.

Decide which words and phrases are not really necessary in each sentence below and cross them out. You can also replace words or change their position to make each sentence more clear and concise. Write the revised sentence.

1. In your own opinion, do you think students should have to wear uniforms?

   _____

2. What is incredible about the cheetah is the cheetah's quickness!

   _____

3. I drew an egg-shaped oval, a round circle, and a four-sided square.

   _____

4. The neighborhood families worked as a team all together.

   _____

5. That elephant is an enormous elephant in size!

   _____

6. The ostrich, the world's largest flightless bird, is a big bird that can run as fast as 40 miles per hour.

   _____

   _____

There is more than one way to revise some of the sentences above. Choose two sentences and revise them in as many different ways as you can on another sheet of paper. Then, read all your revisions. Think about which one seems the most effective and why.

Lots of Words

Do you sometimes run together several ideas into one long, run-on sentence?

According to my grandma, it is a good idea to eat chicken soup when you have a cold and believe it or not, scientists agree with her the soup fights the stuffiness by thinning out the lining of your sinuses.

You can easily fix a run-on sentence by rewriting each complete idea as a separate sentence. Begin each sentence with a capital letter and end it with the correct punctuation mark.

According to my grandma, it is a good idea to eat chicken soup when you have a cold. Believe it or not, scientists agree with her! The soup fights the stuffiness by thinning out the lining of your sinuses.

Rewrite each run-on sentence correctly.

1 Did you know that carrots really are good for your eyes there is a vitamin in this crunchy orange root called beta-carotene that may help lower the risk of eye disease and so the next time you find carrot sticks in your lunch don't trade them or toss them away munch away in good health instead?

_____

_____

_____

_____

2 Think about all the foods you eat and are they nutritious and do they have all the vitamins and minerals your body needs to be healthy, or are they full of fats, sugar, and salt use that information to make healthful choices because you are what you eat.

_____

_____

_____

_____

A Capital Adventure

You know that the first word of a sentence is always capitalized.
Here are more rules on capitalization. Capitalize:

- the names of people and pets.

  My friend, Maggie Ames, has two cats, Hero and Spike.

- titles such as Dr., Mrs., Mr., Miss, and Ms.

  Mr. Ames and Maggie took the cats to Dr. Jones, the vet, last week.

- the names of days, months, and holidays, but not the seasons.

  Maggie got Spike on the Tuesday before Thanksgiving last fall.

- titles of relatives when they are used as a name.

  I can't have a cat because Mom and my sister have allergies.

- names of places, buildings, and monuments.

  *Maggie is in New York City this week. She is going to visit
  the Empire State Building and the Statue of Liberty.*

- direction words when they name a region.

  We live in the Southeast. Maggie and her family flew north yesterday morning.

**Find 15 errors in capitalization below. Some words should be capitalized and some
should not. Mark three lines under each letter that should be capitalized (i).
Draw a line through each letter that should not be capitalized (B).**

   The best time to visit Washington, D.c., is in the early Spring. the weather is just right in
april, not too hot or cold. The cherry blossoms were in bloom while we were there, so that
made my Mom happy! We got to the Capital early monday morning after a ten-hour drive
from the midwest. After checking into our hotel, we decided to visit the national Air and
space Museum first. I could have spent all week there, although the Washington
monument, the Lincoln Memorial, and the White house were really cool. I was hoping to
see the president, but he was in europe. We did see a Senator from our State, though.

Answer each of the following questions. Use capital letters where necessary.

1 In which region of the United States is your home state?

_____

2 What two holidays do people celebrate during the eleventh month of the year?

_____

© Scholastic Inc.

And the Winner Is . . .

Commas let readers know where to pause when reading a sentence. Use a comma:

- after each item in a series of three or more, except after the last item.
  Max wrote, read, and revised his story.

- to set off the name of the person you are addressing directly.
  Will you read it one more time, Jamie?

- after introductory words like yes, no, and well.
  Yes, I have some time right now.

- to set off an appositive (a word or phrase that provides more information about a noun) from the rest of the sentence.
  The Pen to Paper Club, a writers' organization, sponsored a contest.

- before a conjunction that joins two sentences.
  Max entered his story, but he never thought he'd win.

- after a dependent clause that begins a sentence.
  When the letter came, Max was too nervous to open it.

- to set off words that interrupt the basic idea of a sentence.
  Max's sister, therefore, opened it for him.

- to separate geographical names and dates.
  Max won a trip to Orlando, Florida. They left Monday, June 23, 2021.

Write a sentence to answer each question. Include commas where they are needed.

1 On what day and date will you celebrate your next birthday?

_____

2 If you could choose to live in any city or town in any state, where would it be?

_____

3 How would you complete the following sentence?

Whenever I _____

4 Imagine that you have been asked to introduce the president of the United States at a town hall meeting. How would you begin your introduction using direct address?

_____

Listen to the Music

You can use the conjunctions *and, but,* and *or* to combine parts of sentences. When the subjects of two or more sentences share the same verb, you can combine them using *and.* Change the verb form from singular to plural if the subject is plural.

Kyle likes music. Jessie likes music. ⟶ *Kyle and Jessie like music.*

When the objects in two or more sentences are different but share the same subject and predicate, you can also combine them into one sentence.

Kyle can play jazz. Kyle can play rock. ⟶ *Kyle can play jazz and rock.*

When the subjects of two or more sentences are the same but have different predicates, you can combine them into one sentence using *and* and sometimes *but.*

Kyle sings. He plays drums in a band. ⟶ *Kyle sings and plays drums in a band.*

Jessie plays guitar. Jessie doesn't sing. ⟶ *Jessie plays guitar but doesn't sing.*

Complete each pair of sentences. Then, use the rules above to combine them.

1 Many songbirds eat _____. Many songbirds eat _____.

_____

2 You should always _____. You should always _____.

_____

3 A _____ is worth less than a quarter. A _____ is worth less than a quarter.

_____

4 _____ is a famous landmark. _____ is a famous landmark.

_____

5 All living things need _____. All living things need _____.

_____

6 _____ hibernate in winter. _____ hibernate in winter.

_____

7 Many kids enjoy _____. Many kids enjoy _____.

_____

That's Deep!

An **appositive** is a word or phrase that follows a noun or pronoun that explains or identifies what it is or gives more information about it. Commas set off an appositive from the rest of the sentence.

Lake Baikal, the world's deepest lake, is in Siberia, a region of Russia.

If the subjects in two related sentences are the same, you can sometimes combine the sentences by using an appositive.

Sentence 1: *Baikal is also known as the world's oldest freshwater lake.*

Sentence 2: *It dates back about 25 million years.*

Combined: *Baikal, also known as the world's oldest freshwater lake, dates back about 25 million years.*

Underline two sentences in each paragraph that can be combined by using an appositive. Then, write the combined sentence. Remember to include commas.

1   What is the world's most expensive spice? If you guessed saffron, then you are right. Saffron is worth about $2,000 a pound. It takes a long time to harvest saffron. That is why it costs so much.

_____

_____

2   The atlas moth is the world's largest moth. It has a wingspan of about 12 inches. Picture a dinner plate, and you'll have a good idea about how large an atlas moth is. They are so large that people sometimes mistake them for birds when they are in flight. Atlas moths are found in tropical areas.

_____

_____

3   Georgia is the top peanut-producing state in the United States. It harvests more than 2 billion pounds of peanuts each year. Georgia provides about half the peanuts used for making peanut butter. Did you know that our country's 39th president was also a peanut farmer in Plains, Georgia? Jimmy Carter served as president from 1977 to 1981.

_____

_____

Rise and Shine

You can use **subordinate conjunctions** to combine sentences. These words, listed below, can show cause-and-effect and time relationships between the sentences you combine.

since   when   after   unless   because   as   while   before   if   although   until   whenever

The combined sentence will have two parts, an **independent clause** and a **dependent clause**. An independent clause is a full sentence. A dependent clause contains a subject and a verb, but does not express a complete thought. If you put the dependent clause at the beginning of a sentence, follow it with a comma.

Amy fell asleep in class today. She had stayed up too late last night.
independent clause   **dependent clause**
↓   ↓
Amy fell asleep in class today because she had stayed up too late last night.

The bell rang. Amy woke up and realized she had been asleep.
dependent clause   **independent clause**
↓   ↓
When the bell rang, Amy woke up and realized she had been asleep.

. . . .

Combine each pair of sentences. Use one of the subordinate conjunctions from above.

1 Ms. Lee never said a word in class. She knew Amy had been asleep.

_____

2 Amy was walking toward the door. Ms. Lee called her name.

_____

3 Her face turned bright red. She was really embarrassed.

_____

4 Poor Amy tried to calm down. She turned and faced Ms. Lee.

_____

5 Amy explained why she had fallen asleep. She apologized to Ms. Lee.

_____

Time to Experiment

Combining sentences helps to eliminate the problem of short or choppy sentences in paragraphs. You can often combine related sentences into compound sentences by using the conjunctions *and*, *but*, *or*, and *so*. Compare the following two paragraphs. Which is easier to understand?

Young Alva was curious about everything. That curiosity led him to continually ask questions. His mother had been a teacher. She didn't always know the answers. If no one could tell him, he experimented. Once he wanted to know how eggs hatch. He sat on some goose eggs to find out. Can you guess who Alva is? Do you need another hint?

Young Alva was curious about everything, and that curiosity led him to continually ask questions. His mother had been a teacher, but she didn't always know the answers. If no one could tell him, he experimented. Once he wanted to know eggs hatch, so he sat on some goose eggs to find out. Can you guess who Alva is, or do you need another hint?

Read the paragraph below. Place parentheses around the pairs of sentences that can be combined with *and*, *but*, *or*, or *so*. Then, rewrite the paragraph with the combined sentences. Remember to include commas.

My brother Alex has more "interests" than anyone I know. The novelty always wears off very quickly. Last week, Alex wanted to join the school band. He asked if he could rent a drum set. My parents just looked at each other. I knew what they were thinking. Would they be able to convince Alex to try something a little quieter? Would he insist on the drums? Well, they convinced Alex to try something else. It wasn't something quieter. Today he informed us that he's decided to try the tuba. Needless to say, I hope this novelty wears off very, very quickly!

_____

_____

_____

_____

_____

_____

Solve the Problem

Sometimes you can take the important details from several related sentences and combine them into one sentence to make the meaning more clear. Compare the two paragraphs.

> Seagulls can be a problem at the beach. I was trying to eat a sandwich when a gull landed near my blanket. <u>The bird was fearless. It snatched the sandwich out of my hand. It happened suddenly.</u> I couldn't believe it!

Notice how choppy the three underlined sentences are in the above paragraph.

> Seagulls can be a problem at the beach. I was trying to eat a sandwich when a gull landed near my blanket. <u>The fearless bird suddenly snatched the sandwich right out of my hand.</u> I couldn't believe it!

By combining the information into one sentence, you can solve the problem of short, choppy sentences, improve your writing, and make the sentence more clear.

Read each paragraph. Put a box around the groups of sentences with details that can be combined into one sentence. Look for other ways to combine sentences as well. Then, rewrite the paragraph with the changes.

My grandfather has a motorboat. It is small. It is called a runabout. He keeps it at a marina. The marina is nearby. Gramps took me crabbing one morning. It was before sunrise. I was half asleep. My job was tying fish heads to the lines. The fish heads were smelly. That sure woke me up. It was worth it. We caught crabs. They were blue. We caught six dozen. What a great dinner we had that night!

_____

_____

_____

_____

_____

_____

Powerful Paragraphs

A **paragraph** is a group of sentences that focuses on a topic and one main idea about that topic. A **topic sentence** expresses that main idea. It may answer *who, what, where, when, why, how,* or a combination of questions. Although a topic sentence often begins a paragraph, it can come at the end or even in the middle of a paragraph. The other sentences in the paragraph develop the main idea by telling more about it. They are called supporting sentences.

. . . .

Read the paragraphs. Underline the topic sentence in each. Circle each supporting sentence. Then, write the question or questions that each topic sentence answers.

1. There is an energizing chill in the air now that the days are shorter. The last of the crops are about to be harvested, and a blanket of leaves covers much of the landscape. All but a few of our summertime visitors have already flown south for warmer places. Once again, the long, hot days of summer have given way to fall.

_____

_____

2. Falling asleep was never a problem for me until we moved to the country. I was used to the sounds of subway trains pulling into the station near our apartment, the horns and squealing brakes of buses, taxis, and cars, wailing sirens, and planes landing or taking off. I was not used to the sound of chirping crickets. My parents assured me that I would get used to it. They were right, of course, but it took awhile.

_____

_____

3. An amazing marsupial spends up to 22 hours a day asleep in a eucalyptus tree. A nocturnal creature, it is mostly active at night. The habits of the world's sleepiest animal, the koala, really fascinate me. When it is awake, the koala feeds on eucalyptus leaves and shoots, up to two pounds at a time. What's more, it seldom drinks water because it gets most of what it needs from the leaves and shoots.

_____

_____

Grab Some Attention

A **topic sentence** expresses the main idea about the topic of a paragraph. It should tell just enough to interest your readers. Remember that it may answer *who*, *what*, *where*, *when*, *why*, or *how*, or a combination of questions. Here is an example.

Topic:	an accident on a space station
Topic Sentence:	An alarm shattered the silence, alerting the crew that something was terribly wrong.

For each topic, write a topic sentence that would grab the attention of your readers.

1 **Topic:** a frightening experience

Topic Sentence: _____

2 **Topic:** wearing uniforms to school, yes or no

Topic Sentence: _____

3 **Topic:** why the opossum has no hair on its tail

Topic Sentence: _____

4 **Topic:** witnessing a friend steal a candy bar

Topic Sentence: _____

Come up with some topics of your own. Then, write a topic sentence for each one.

1 Topic: _____

Topic Sentence: _____

2 Topic: _____

Topic Sentence: _____

3 Topic: _____

Topic Sentence: _____

4 Topic: _____

Topic Sentence: _____

The Mighty End

No matter what your purpose for writing—to inform, persuade, or entertain—or what form your writing takes—story, news report, explanation, letter to an editor, or personal narrative—try to include a strong ending sentence. The ending sentence in a paragraph is called the **closing sentence**. It retells the topic sentence in a new way. It can be a surprise or an unexpected solution. It can ask a question or answer a question. It can explain or teach something. Here are some examples.

Aren't you glad you didn't live back then?

To this day, the mystery of the disappearing statue has never been solved.

That's what they told us, but we knew better!

So, be careful what you wish for because it just may happen.

Would you want to eat at that restaurant?

Unfortunately, we still had three more hours to go!

Write a strong closing sentence for each writing situation below.

1 a news report about an earthquake or tornado

_____

2 an account of a UFO sighting

_____

3 an explanation of how to study for a history test

_____

4 an ad for a nutritious cereal you have developed

_____

5 a warning about skateboarding without the proper equipment

_____

6 a lesson on how to make the perfect submarine sandwich

_____

In the Know

You know that a paragraph should have a topic sentence that expresses the main idea of the paragraph. Here is a topic sentence from a story.

*Malcolm could never have imagined the incredible
journey he was about to make.*

Who is Malcolm? Where will his journey take him? Why is it incredible? What will happen? Whom will he meet?

These are just a few of the questions you may ask after reading the topic sentence. You can use the answers to questions like these to develop supporting details for the paragraphs you write.

Read each topic sentence. Write questions you would want the paragraph to answer.

1 So faint was the sound that Emerald thought it was just the rustling of leaves.

_____

_____

_____

2 Aliyah realized that there was only one way to end the ridiculous argument.

_____

_____

_____

3 Max thought baking a birthday cake was a "piece of cake," but he was wrong!

_____

_____

_____

4 They're fun to ride, they're completely portable, and millions of kids ride them every day.

_____

_____

Choose and rewrite one of the topic sentences on page 20. Then, reread the
questions you listed and use your imagination to answer them. Use your answers
to write supporting sentences for a possible paragraph. Add any other details that
you think of to support the topic.

Topic Sentence: _____

_____

Supporting Sentences:

- _____

_____

- _____

_____

- _____

_____

- _____

_____

Now, use the information to write a paragraph. Include a closing sentence.
Remember to indent, capitalize, and punctuate correctly.

_____

_____

_____

_____

_____

_____

_____

_____

A Scrumptious Topic

Before you write a first draft of a paragraph, take the time to think about the topic and to review the facts, details, and ideas you have written.

Read the topic and the notes for a paragraph about the world's best hot fudge sundae. Cross out the details which seem unnecessary or unrelated. Then, read the three possible topic sentences. Make a check next to the best topic sentence.

Topic: the world's best hot fudge sundae

Details:
- at least 3 scoops of vanilla ice cream, should fill bowl—a big bowl
- mounds of fresh-whipped heavy cream—slightly sweetened
- need napkins
- big spoonful or 2 to 3 spoons of chopped walnuts
- lots and lots of hot fudge, has to be thick and gooey
- a couple of cherries on top with a little cherry juice
- hot, cold, sweet, crunchy, creamy, and yummy all in one
- meant to be shared with a friend—or not
- don't forget the spoon
- perfect dessert for ice cream lovers—young and old
- serve with a glass of water

Possible topic sentences:

There is absolutely nothing more scrumptious than my hot fudge sundae recipe.
The hardest part of making a hot fudge sundae is not eating it as you make it.
If you like ice cream, you'll love my recipe for a hot fudge sundae.

Number the details above to show the order in which you would use them. The order should make sense. Then, use the details to write supporting sentences in order below.

_____

_____

_____

_____

_____

_____

_____

Now, choose one of the following topics, or one of your own, and follow the steps.

friendship	making a BLT on toast	a great hobby
a superstition	a musical instrument	a mystery gift

- Write the topic and list at least three details about it.
- Review your list. Cross out any details that do not relate to the topic. Add any other details that are important. Number the details in an order that makes sense.
- Write two possible topic sentences. Check the one that best tells the main idea.

Topic: _____

Details: _____

_____

_____

_____

Possible topic sentences:

_____

_____

Use the topic and details from above to write the first draft of a paragraph. Begin by writing the topic sentence that best tells the main idea. Then, add the details that best support your topic sentence.

_____

_____

_____

_____

_____

Now proofread your first draft. Do the sentences support the topic sentence? Are they in an order that makes sense? Are they clearly written and interesting? Do they begin and end correctly? Revise your paragraph. Make the necessary changes. Then, rewrite the paragraph on another sheet of paper.

Read Carefully

When you **proofread** your work, you look for errors and mark them so that you can correct them. Here are some marks you can use when you proofread your work.

delete	The ~~the~~ phone rang.
insert a word	The ^phone^ rang.
insert a comma	The phone rang, and I answered it.
insert quotation marks	A voice said, "Hello."
insert a period	The phone rang.
insert an apostrophe	It's ringing again.
close up space	The ph one rang.
insert a space	The phone rang.
switch order of letters	The phone ragn.
capitalize	the phone rang.
make lowercase	The pHone rang.
start new paragraph	¶ The phone rang.

Read the following part of a story. Proofread it using the marks above. There are 13 errors.

The most amazing thing happened this morning. I still can't believe it! Just as I was about to fill one of my feeders, I noticed a Chickadee perched on the lower branch of a nearby tree   The little bird seemed to be watching me. Of course, chickadees really like like sunflower seeds and that's what I always put in this feeder. I figured it was probably hungry and just waiting for me to finish up and leave. It was then that I got this great idea.

Chicadees are supposed to be easy to hand tame. well, the chickadee was still perched on the, and I had the seeds, so I decided to try. I took a bunch of seeds, held out my hand—palm up—next to the feeder and stood very still. I didnt even scra tch my nose when it started to itch! About a minutelater, the chickadee flew to the tree closest to the feeder. I held my breath and waited. The didn't fly to my hand, but it did fly to the feeder! It took a seed and flew off to eat it. I knew it wuold be back, so I continued to watch and wait

Working Together

Illustrations and photographs often contain important and interesting details that you can use to write a story, an article, an essay, or just a simple paragraph.

Look at the illustration. Think about the details it shows and what you can write about. Then, write a possible topic sentence for the illustration.

_____

Write details about the illustration that support your topic sentence.

_____

_____

_____

_____

Review your ideas. Then, write a brief paragraph about the illustration. Include a closing sentence.

_____

_____

_____

_____

_____

_____

Make It Exact

You can make your writing more interesting and exciting by choosing and replacing overused, inexact words.

Big waves hit the land along the sea during the storm.
Gigantic waves battered the coast during the hurricane.

Keep a thesaurus handy when you write and revise your writing.

Replace each deleted word with a more exact, colorful, or interesting word. Write it above the word. Then, rewrite each sentence with the changes you made.

1 The ~~loud~~ siren ~~told~~ residents to take shelter immediately.

_____

2 The ~~tired~~ hikers nearly collapsed after the ~~hard~~ trek.

_____

3 My opponent may be ~~small,~~ but what a ~~strong~~ serve she delivers!

_____

4 What is the name of that ~~bright~~ blue bird ~~sitting~~ on the feeder?

_____

5 The men ~~stopped~~ as the rattler ~~moved~~ across their path.

_____

6 The audience ~~laughed~~ at the comedian's ~~funny~~ stories.

_____

 Just for fun, on another sheet of paper, rewrite a portion of a familiar children's story such as "Little Red Riding Hood." Replace any overused and inexact words with more interesting, exciting words.

It's All Business!

There are many reasons for writing a business letter. You might request information, express an opinion, or explain a problem you have. A business letter has six parts:

- The **heading** gives your address and the date.
- The **inside address** gives the name and address of the person or company receiving the letter. It can include the person's title.

- A **formal greeting,** such as *Dear Sir:,* comes next. It can include a title of respect, such as Ms., Mrs., or Mr.
- The **body** states the purpose of your letter.
- A **formal closing,** such as *Sincerely yours,* follows the body.
- Your **signature** is last.

Imagine that you bought a popular new toy from the Razzle-Dazzle Toy Company. Unfortunately, the toy broke on the first day! Would you want your money back? Would you want a replacement? Write a letter to the company at 123 Any Street, Anytown, Anystate, 00001. Explain why you are writing. Tell what happened and how. Then, suggest a solution to the problem.

heading → _____

_____ ← inside address   _____

_____   _____

_____

_____ : ← formal greeting   body
                                            ↓

_____

_____

_____

_____

_____

formal closing → _____

signature → _____

The Power of Persuasion

Have you ever tried to convince someone to feel the way you do about something?
To write a convincing **persuasive paragraph**, state your opinion clearly, give reasons,
and support your opinion with facts. Remember that facts can be checked or proven.

Dear Editor:

Our town should consider building a skateboard park. According to a recent
community survey, there are more kids skateboarding than ever before but fewer places
to skateboard. Certain townspeople and merchants have complained to authorities that
skateboarders make too much noise, create a nuisance for pedestrians and drivers, and
are causing property damage. As a result, we skateboarders are continually "asked" to
move on. We are always looking for new places to practice. Specially designated areas
and parks for skateboarders have worked in other communities with similar problems.
If everyone would work together, it could work here.

Jason Anderson

Green Hills

1. Underline Jason's opinion.
2. Circle the reasons Jason gives for his opinion.
3. Highlight the facts that support his reasons.

. . . .

**Think about a problem that you feel deeply about. What is your opinion?
Write what you think should be done to resolve the problem or issue.**

_____

List reasons for your opinion.   **List facts to support your opinion.**

_____   _____

_____   _____

_____   _____

**Write a persuasive paragraph on another sheet of paper. Ask a friend to read it.
Does he or she agree or disagree with you? Does your friend have suggestions that
could improve your paragraph to make it more persuasive? Revise your paragraph.**

Step by Step

Whenever you write about something that has happened or how to do or to make something, it is important to write about the events or the steps in the correct order.

Carefully read the notes about the day the Mason family went on vacation. Number the events in the order that they happened.

_____ back on road by 1:00

_____ stopped for lunch around noon

_____ helped Dad load up the van

_____ unloaded van and went down to the beach

_____ up at 6:00 a.m., got dressed, ate breakfast

_____ double-checked house before locking up

_____ stopped for gas on way out of town

_____ arrived at the motel by late afternoon

_____ got on the turnpike and headed east

_____ piled in the van and ready to go by 7:30

Pretend that the notes above are yours. Use them to write a paragraph. Include a topic sentence, closing sentence, and title. Write about the events in sequence. Remember to begin and end each sentence correctly. You may want to include words such as *before*, *that*, *after*, *first*, *next*, *then*, *later*, and *finally* to help indicate the order in which you did things. Use another sheet of paper, if needed.

_____

_____

_____

_____

_____

Finding the Way

A **how-to paragraph** gives directions for doing or making something. It usually includes a topic sentence, any necessary materials, and step-by-step directions. Writers often use time-order words and phrases such as *first, next, then, after that,* and *finally* to help indicate the sequence. The directions in the paragraph below are not very clear.

Do you turn left or right at the light?

How many blocks are "a few" blocks?

Which street?

Getting from school to my house is a snap. Just walk a few blocks down the street toward town. Turn at the traffic light. Go a couple more blocks. My house is on the corner. If you go past the intersection, you've gone too far.

Which corner?

Which intersection is too far?

How many blocks are "a couple more" blocks?

Think about how to get from your home to the library. Sketch the route in the box below. Then, write a paragraph with clear and specific directions. Include the names of streets and buildings, direction words such as *left, right, north, south, east,* and *west,* and time-order words.

From _____ to _____

_____

_____

_____

_____

Definitely Dynamic

A **definition paragraph** is similar to a word definition except that it is much more detailed. You not only define the word, but you include details that answer questions such as: *What is it like? What purpose does it serve? Where or when do you use it? What does it look like? Does it make or have a sound? What does it feel like? Does It have a taste? Does it smell? What does it do?*

List several common nouns. Here are a few to get you started.

home	sneakers	_____	_____
pencil	skateboard	_____	_____
helmet	key	_____	_____

· ·

Choose three words. Look up each one in a dictionary and write the definition.

_____ : _____

_____ : _____

_____ : _____

· ·

Now, write a short definition paragraph for one of the words that not only tells what it is but also includes details that answer some of the questions above. Remember to include a topic sentence and a closing sentence. Use your imagination and creativity.

_____

_____

_____

_____

_____

_____

Read and Review

A **book review** is an analysis of a book you have read that includes facts and opinions supported by reasons. It has three parts: The **introduction** is a paragraph that begins with an attention-grabbing topic sentence. The **body** includes a summary of the plot and information about the setting and main characters. The **conclusion** can include a hint about the ending and your opinions.

Complete the book-review planner about a book you have recently read.
Then, use the information to write your book review on another sheet of paper.

Title: _____   Author: _____

Type of Book (science fiction, realistic fiction, mystery, etc.): _____

Main Character(s): _____

_____

Setting (where, when): _____

Plot (main events, problem/solution): _____

_____

Special Features (illustrations/photographs, language, diary/journal entries):

_____

Opinions

The character(s) I liked most and why: _____

How I would describe the plot—interesting, exciting, boring, so-so—and why:

_____

The part of the book I enjoyed most (least) and why: _____

_____

Features of the book I liked (disliked) and why: _____

_____

Why I would (would not) recommend this book: _____

_____

A Great Way to Organize

An **outline** is a great way to organize your ideas before
you write. Each main idea becomes a paragraph with a topic
sentence and facts and details that support the main idea.

Prepare to write your autobiography, the story of your life,
using the outline form below. For numerals I and II, list details
that tell about each main idea. For numeral III, come up with
another possible main idea, such as important influences, major events, facts
about your family, or influential people, and then list details. Then, use the outline
to write your autobiography on another sheet of paper.

All About Me → main topic

I. Biographical Facts → Main Idea 1

   A. _____ facts and details

   B. _____

   C. _____

   D. _____

II. My Major Accomplishments → Main Idea 2

   A. _____ facts and details

   B. _____

   C. _____

   D. _____

III. _____ → Main Idea 3

   A. _____ facts and details

   B. _____

   C. _____

   D. _____

Getting Organized

When you are getting ready to write two or more paragraphs for a report, you can make the task easier if you follow these steps:

• Organize related facts and details into groups.

• Write a topic sentence expressing the main idea for each group.

• Use the facts and details in each group to write sentences that support each topic sentence.

The Dead Sea is a saltwater lake located between Israel and Jordan. Read the facts below about the Dead Sea and organize them into three groups for a report. Think of a category name for each group of facts. Then, use ✱s, ✔s, and ✘s to indicate the facts that belong in each group.

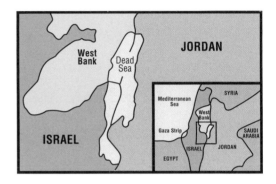

✱ = _____

✔ = _____

✘ = _____

_____ ① one of the saltiest bodies of water in world

_____ ② covers about 400 square miles

_____ ③ almost impossible for swimmers to sink in Dead Sea because of high density of salt

_____ ④ water comes from Jordan River and streams

_____ ⑤ measures about 11 miles wide at widest point

_____ ⑥ water so salty that fish die immediately; nothing but simple microorganisms survive in Dead Sea

_____ ⑦ measures about 31 miles long

_____ ⑧ bottom measures to depths of 2,622 feet below sea level

_____ ⑨ water doesn't flow out of Dead Sea

_____ ⑩ water evaporates, leaving salt and other minerals behind

Write a topic sentence for each group of facts about the Dead Sea.
Then, use the facts to write sentences that support each topic sentence.

Subject: **The Dead Sea**

Topic Sentence for Paragraph 1: _____

_____

Supporting Sentences:

_____

_____

_____

_____

Topic Sentence for Paragraph 2: _____

_____

Supporting Sentences:

_____

_____

_____

_____

Topic Sentence for Paragraph 3: _____

_____

Supporting Sentences:

_____

_____

_____

_____

The Narrator

Every story has a **narrator**. When you choose to tell a story from a **first-person** point of view, the narrator is a character who uses the pronouns *I*, *me*, and *myself* to tell what he or she thinks, feels, and does. The readers see the story through the eyes of this character.

I was terrified to see a spider crawling on my shoe. "Matt," I croaked, barely able to speak, "please help me!" Matt turned around and raced to my side.

When you choose to tell a story from a **third-person** point of view, the narrator is not a character but rather someone outside the story. Your narrator reveals the actions and words of all the characters but tells the thoughts and feelings of only one main character.

She was terrified to see a spider crawling on her shoe. "Matt," she croaked, barely able to speak, "please help me!" Matt turned around and raced to her side.

Rewrite the following passage from a first-person point of view.

1   Spotting the doe in a clearing, he froze in his tracks and quietly took out his camera. He didn't want to startle the animal before getting at least one shot. Sensing his presence, the doe looked up at him. "Don't be frightened," he said in his most soothing voice. "I won't hurt you. I just want to take your picture."

_____

_____

_____

_____

Rewrite the following passage from a third-person point of view.

2   After hiking for more than an hour up the steep trail, I decided to take a break because my feet were killing me. Although I had worn my new hiking boots around the house all week, I soon realized that they were not sufficiently broken in. "I should have listened to Beth and worn my old boots," I grumbled to myself.
    "Did you say something, Jenny?" Beth asked.

_____

_____

_____

_____

Look at the scenario below. Write a short story using the first-person point of view—either the camper's or the skunk's. A topic sentence is provided to help you get started.

It was an absolutely perfect summer evening at the Pine Grove Campground until my

unexpected encounter _____

_____

_____

_____

_____

Now, rewrite the story using the third-person point of view.

It was an absolutely perfect summer evening at the Pine Grove Campground until the

unexpected encounter _____

_____

_____

_____

_____

Choose a favorite fairy tale, such as "Little Red Riding Hood," "Goldilocks and the Three Bears," or "Jack and the Beanstalk." For fun, on another sheet of paper, rewrite the story as a first-person narrative, as if you were one of the characters.

Make a Plan

It helps to plan a story before writing. A plan will help you determine characters, the setting (where and when the story takes place), and the plot (all the actions or events in the story). The plot includes a problem, events leading to the climax, or most exciting part of the story, and events leading to the resolution.

. . . .

What kinds of stories do you like? Do you prefer historical fiction or realistic fiction, action adventures or mysteries? Answer the questions below to plan a story you think your friends will enjoy. Then, write a draft of your story on another sheet of paper.

What is the title? _____

Where and when will the story take place? _____

Describe the main character. _____

What problem(s) will your main character face? _____

_____

What other characters will you include? _____

What will be the most exciting moment or turning point? _____

_____

What events or actions will lead up to this moment? _____

_____

What events or actions will follow this moment and show how the problem is resolved?

_____

_____

What is the resolution? _____

_____

Will you tell your story in the first-person or third-person point of view? _____

_____

Time to Talk

When you include dialogue in a story, use quotation marks around the speaker's exact words. Use a comma to set off the quotation from the rest of the sentence. Place end punctuation marks and commas inside the quotation marks.

Ben grumbled, "I can't find my sneakers."

"You're always misplacing something," commented his sister Janelle.

If a quotation is a question, end it with a question mark. If a quotation is an exclamation, end it with an exclamation mark.

"Where did you take them off?" asked Mrs. Abbot, trying to be helpful.

"Just follow the smell!" teased his brother.

If a quotation is divided but still one sentence, use commas to separate the quote from the words that tell who the speaker is.

"You may think you're a comedian," replied Ben, "but you're not funny."

If a quotation is divided and two separate sentences, place a period after the words that identify the speaker. Then, begin the second sentence with a capital letter.

"I'm sorry," Sam apologized. "Your sneakers are on the back porch."

Read the following part of a story. Add the missing quotation marks, commas, and end punctuations.

It was Saturday morning, and Janelle was already in the kitchen.

Breakfast will be ready in about five minutes Janelle yelled up to her brothers

Do you want some help offered Mom, who had just walked into the kitchen

Thanks, Mom replied Janelle but I'd really like to do it myself

Okay agreed Mom I'll just take the dog for a quick walk then.

Janelle popped the bread into the toaster and went back to the stove to check on the eggs and bacon

About a minute later, Ben said to Sam Do you smell something burning

Yup answered Sam It smells like burnt toast to me, and there goes the smoke alarm

I guess Janelle's making breakfast again laughed Ben, as they ran down to the kitchen

Do you want some help, Janelle Ben and Sam asked.

The Tone of Talk

When you include dialogue in your writing, do you usually use *said* to signal the words of your speakers? You can make your writing more interesting and effective with words other than *said*. Compare the two versions of the same dialogue.

"I'm tired," said Benny. ⟶ *"I'm tired," <u>whined</u> Benny.*

"Are we almost there?" said Lisa. ⟶ *"Are we almost there?" <u>grumbled</u> Lisa.*

"It'll be another hour," Dad said. ⟶ *"It'll be another hour," Dad <u>promised</u>.*

The words *whined, grumbled, and promised* indicate the feelings and tone of voice of the speakers and make the dialogue more interesting to read.

. . . .

Read each sentence. List the feelings of each speaker. Consider each speaker's words and the word that signaled them.

1 "Silence!" <u>bellowed</u> Dad. _____

2 "That wasn't my intention," <u>admitted</u> Lisa. _____

3 "What was that?" the child <u>whispered</u>. _____

4 "It's not that difficult," my friend <u>assured</u> me. _____

5 "I can't believe you guys!" Jody <u>chuckled</u>. _____

Read the incomplete dialogue. Think about the word that signals each speaker's words. Then, write what you think each speaker said.

My brother Jules is three years younger than I am, but he always wants to tag along with me.

"_____," <u>insisted</u> Jules.

"_____," I <u>muttered</u>, as I tried to leave without getting into an argument.

"_____" he <u>countered</u>, grabbing his baseball glove.

"_____," I <u>yelled</u>, walking toward my bike.

"_____," <u>interrupted</u> Mom.

Look back at the previous page. Underline all the words that were used in place of *said*. Here are more words you can use. Think about what each might indicate about the feelings of a speaker or a speaker's tone of voice. Then, complete each dialogue below by adding a word that you think best signals each speaker's words.

accused	explained	mumbled	quoted	suggested
argued	gasped	objected	refused	teased
balked	giggled	ordered	reported	urged
consoled	hesitated	persuaded	replied	wailed
corrected	hissed	pleaded	roared	whimpered
demanded	instructed	predicted	scolded	wondered
exclaimed	joked	proposed	sobbed	yelped

"Don't be too obvious, but check out that boy in the blue jacket," _____ Jackie to her friends. "He just took a magazine and stuffed it inside his jacket."

"I didn't see him do it," _____ Nirvana.

"Me either," _____ Jessica.

"You really should tell the store manager," _____ Mattie.

"I don't know," _____ Jackie. "What do you think, Jessica?"

"You don't have to do anything," she _____. "It looks like someone else saw him and reported it."

· ·

"Have you ever seen anything so incredible?" _____ Juan.

"There must be thousands of them," he _____ , pointing to the cloud of monarch butterflies flying overhead.

"There are," _____ his grandfather.

"Where are they going?" _____ Juan.

"Every fall," _____ Juan's grandfather, "millions of monarchs migrate from Canada and parts of the United States to Mexico for the winter. Some travel up to 2,000 miles."

"Wow!" _____ Juan.

Grab Some Interest

You can often expand a simple paragraph in a story, article, essay, report, or whatever you are writing and make it more interesting by:

- combining short, choppy sentences.

- adding details to help create a picture, mood, or feeling.

- replacing dull, overused, or inexact nouns, verbs, and adjectives.

- changing the order of words in sentences.

- adding words or phrases such as *also, first, meanwhile, in fact, however, eventually,* and *in the end* to connect ideas or events.

• •

Expand and rewrite each of the paragraphs using some of the suggestions above.

It began to snow. I was surprised. It was the end of April. The temperature had fallen. Clouds began moving in. I knew a storm was coming. Would it be a snowstorm? I woke up the next morning. Snow covered the ground. There would be no baseball practice today!

_____

_____

_____

_____

_____

Something smelled good. We had just passed the bakery. We looked at each other. We smiled. We headed back to the bakery. Erin opened the door. We went inside. What a sight! There were all kinds of goodies. There were breads and rolls. Some were just out of the oven. I went from case to case. Everything looked and smelled good. It was a hard decision. Finally, I chose.

_____

_____

_____

_____

_____

Figuratively Speaking

Figurative language can be used to add details to sentences, to clarify a point, or to enhance your writing. **Metaphors**, **similes**, **hyperbole**, and **personification** are four kinds of figurative language.

A **simile** makes a comparison between two unlike things, using *like* or *as*.

Simon was mad as a hornet after discovering his bike had been stolen.

A **metaphor** makes a comparison between two unlike things, without using *like* or *as*.

The fog was a thick gray blanket covering the entire valley.

Personification gives human characteristics and qualities to nonhuman things like animals and objects.

The moon peeked through the clouds and smiled down on us.

Hyperbole is deliberate exaggeration.

The tension was so thick you could cut it with a knife.

Complete each sentence with a simile, metaphor, hyperbole, or personification. Try to use each type of figurative language at least once. Write *S*, *M*, *P*, or *H* before each sentence to label each figure of speech.

_____ 1 Everyone was so exhausted by the end of the day that _____

_____

_____ 2 Slowly meandering through the countryside, the river _____

_____

_____ 3 The frigid winter air _____

_____

_____ 4 The dilapidated house at the end of the lane _____

_____

_____ 5 Suddenly, the players became _____

_____

_____ 6 Our refrigerator _____

_____

Writing Wonderful Words

Two other kinds of figurative language are **alliteration** and **assonance**. They can also make your stories and poems fun and interesting. **Alliteration** is the repetition of a consonant sound at the beginning of words.

Benjamin Barker loves to bake
Buns and biscuits and buttery cakes,
Breads and brownies and blackberry pies,
Apple brown betty and berry surprise!

Assonance is the repetition of the same vowel sounds either at the beginning of words or inside the words.

Anna's nana asked for bananas and apples—just a few!
And apricots and anchovies and abalone stew!
Antipasto with avocados and ash bread! PHEW!

Underline the letters used to make alliteration or assonance in each group of words below. Choose one example of each and list additional words with the same repeated consonant or vowel sound.

Phyllis the famous photographer	abruptly announced	bellowing yellow yak
everyone excitedly exclaimed	perfect piece of pie	obstinate tot named Otto
impudent imp implored	creepy crawly critter	whittled and whistled

_____   _____

_____   _____   _____   _____

_____   _____   _____   _____

Use the words you listed above to write silly sentences or a poem on the lines below.

_____   _____

_____   _____

_____   _____

_____   _____

Crack! Splat!

When you want readers to "hear" something you are describing, you can use words that imitate the sound it makes. This use of words is called **onomatopoeia**.

The teakettle hissed as the water came to a boil.

As the blazing campfire crackled, it warmed the chilled campers.

Read aloud each word listed below. What comes to mind? Add to the list of words that imitate sounds. To help you get started, answer these questions: What does your stomach do when you are hungry? What does a glass do when it breaks? What does falling rain do on a tin roof?

tick tock _____ _____

hum _____ _____

fizz _____ _____

meow _____ _____

· ·

Use onomatopoeia to complete each sentence below.
Try to use some of the words from your list.

1 The dried leaves _____ underfoot as we walked through the woods.

2 The subway _____ to a stop as it pulled into the station.

3 The cat's sharp claws _____ the upholstery to shreds.

4 The racing car _____ by at 140 miles per hour.

5 The well-oiled machine _____ quietly in the background.

6 The windows _____ noisily as the wind grew stronger.

7 Some of the floorboards and wooden steps in our house are loose, so they

_____ when you walk on them.

8 The siren _____, warning both drivers and

pedestrians along the busy street to make a path for the approaching ambulance.

ANSWER KEY

Page 5
Possible sentences:
Humans breathe twenty times per minute. Count how many times you breathe. How fast you breathe! Is the body really sixty-five percent water? The body is about sixty-five percent water. Believe it. I don't believe it is sixty-five percent water!

Page 6
Lists and sentences will vary.

Page 7
Possible sentences:
1. The students in the bleachers cheered for their team.
2. The saleswoman sold shirts with rainbows on them to the tourists.
3. Dad taught me to read when I was a preschooler.
4. While we were wading in the shallow water, porpoises were swimming just 20 feet away from us.
5. The dog started barking at me while I was emptying the dishwasher this morning.
6. On the news today, we heard about the missing painting that was found.

Page 8
Possible answers:
1. Do you think students should have to wear uniforms?
2. The cheetah's quickness is incredible.
3. I drew an oval, a circle, and a square.
4. The neighborhood families worked as a team.
5. That elephant is enormous!
6. The ostrich, the world's largest flightless bird, can run up to 40 miles per hour.

Page 9
1. Did you know that carrots really are good for your eyes? There is a vitamin in this crunchy orange root called beta-carotene that may help lower the risk of eye disease. The next time you find carrot sticks in your lunch, don't trade them or toss them away. Munch away in good health instead.
2. Think about all the foods you eat. Are they nutritious? Do they have all the vitamins and minerals your body needs to be healthy, or are they full of fats, sugar, and salt? Use that information to make healthful choices because you are what you eat.

Page 10
The best time to visit Washington, D.C., is in the early spring. The weather is just right in April, not too hot or cold. The cherry blossoms were in bloom while we were there, so that made my mom happy! We got to the capital early Monday morning after a ten-hour drive from the Midwest. After checking into our hotel, we decided to visit the National Air and Space Museum first. I could have spent all week there, although the Washington Monument, the Lincoln Memorial, and the White House were really cool. I was hoping to see the president, but he was in Europe. We did see a senator from our state, though.
1. Answers will vary.
2. Possible answers: Veteran's Day, Thanksgiving Day

Page 11
Answers will vary.

Page 12
Answers will vary.

Page 13
Possible sentences:
1. If you guessed saffron, worth about $2,000 a pound, then you are right.
2. The atlas moth, the world's largest moth, has a wingspan of about 12 inches.,
3. Georgia, the top peanut-producing state in the United States, harvests more than 2 billion pounds of peanuts each year.

Page 14
Possible sentences:
1. Ms. Lee never said a word in class although she knew Amy had been asleep.
2. As Amy was walking toward the door, Ms. Lee called her name.
3. Her face turned bright red because she was really embarrassed.
4. Poor Amy tried to calm down as she turned and faced Ms. Lee.
5. After Amy explained why she had fallen asleep, she apologized to Ms. Lee.

Page 15
My brother Alex has more "interests" than anyone I know, but the novelty always wears off very quickly. Last week, Alex wanted to join the school band, so he asked if he could rent a drum set. My parents just looked at each other. I knew what they were thinking. Would they be able to convince Alex to try something a little quieter, or would he insist on the drums? Well, they convinced Alex to try something else, but it wasn't something quieter. Today he informed us that he's decided to try the tuba. Needless to say, I hope this novelty wears off very, very, very quickly!

Page 16
Possible paragraph: My grandfather has a small motorboat called a runabout. He keeps it at a nearby marina. Gramps took me crabbing one morning. It was before sunrise, and I was half asleep. My job, tying smelly fish heads to the lines, sure woke me up. But it was worth it because we caught six dozen blue crabs. What a great dinner we had that night!

Page 17
1. There is an energizing chill in the air now that the days are shorter. The last of the crops are about to be harvested, and a blanket of leaves covers much of the landscape. All but a few of our summertime visitors have already flown south for warmer places. Once again, the long, hot days of summer have given way to fall.
Questions: What has happened? When?

2. Falling asleep was never a problem for me until we moved to the country. I was used to the sounds of subway trains pulling into the station near our apartment, the horns and squealing brakes of buses, taxis, and cars, wailing sirens, and planes landing or taking off. I was not used to the sounds of chirping crickets. My parents assured me that I would get used to it. They were right, of course, but it took awhile.
Questions: Who? When? What? Where?

3. This amazing marsupial spends up to 22 hours a day asleep in a eucalyptus tree. A nocturnal creature, it is mostly active at night. The habits of the world's sleepiest animal, the koala, really fascinate me. When it is awake, the koala feeds on eucalyptus leaves and shoots, up to two pounds at a time. What's more, it seldom drinks water because it gets most of what it needs from the leaves and shoots.
Questions: What? Who?

Page 18
Topics and topic sentences will vary.

Page 19
Closing sentences will vary.

Page 20
Questions will vary. Possible responses:
1. Who is Emerald? What was making the sound that Emerald heard? What will Emerald do?
2. Who is Aliyah? With whom has she been arguing? What is the argument about? How will she settle the argument?
3. Why was Max baking a birthday cake? For whom was he baking the cake? Why did he think it was a "piece of cake" at first? What caused him to realize that baking a birthday cake wasn't a "piece of cake"? How was the cake?
4. What things are fun to ride? In what way are they portable? Who are the millions of kids that ride them every day?

Page 21
Topic sentences, supporting sentences, and paragraphs will vary.

Page 22
Possible unrelated details: need napkins, meant to be shared with a friend—or not, don't forget the spoon, perfect dessert for ice cream lovers—young and old, serve with a glass of water
Possible order of details:
1. at least 3 scoops of vanilla ice cream, should fill bowl—a big bowl
2. lots and lots of hot fudge, has to be thick and gooey
3. mounds of fresh-whipped heavy cream—slightly sweetened
4. big spoonful or 2 to 3 spoons of chopped walnuts
5. a couple of cherries on top with a little cherry juice
6. hot, cold, sweet, crunchy, creamy, and yummy all in one
Supporting sentences will vary.

Page 23
Topics, details, topic sentences, and paragraphs will vary.

Page 24
The most amazing thing happened this morning. I still can't believe it! Just as I was about to fill one of my feeders, I noticed a chickadee perched on the lower branch of a nearby tree. The little bird seemed to be watching me. Of course, chickadees really like sunflower seeds, and that's what I always put in this feeder. I figured it was probably hungry and just waiting for me to finish up and leave. It was then that I got this great idea.

Chickadees are supposed to be easy to hand tame. Well, the chickadee was still perched on the branch, and I had the seeds, so I decided to try. I took a bunch of seeds, held out my hand—palm up—next to the feeder, and stood very still. I didn't even scratch my nose when it started to itch! About a minute later, the chickadee flew to the tree closest to the feeder. I held my breath and waited. The chickadee didn't fly to my hand, but it did fly to the feeder! It took a seed and flew off to eat it. I knew it would be back, so I continued to watch and wait.

Page 25
Answers will vary.

Page 26
Answers will vary.

Page 27
Letters will vary.

Page 28
Our town should consider building a skateboard park. According to a recent community survey, there are more kids skateboarding than ever before but fewer places to skateboard. Certain townspeople and merchants have complained that skateboarders make too much noise and create a nuisance for pedestrians and drivers. As a result, we skateboarders are continually "asked" to move on. We are always looking for new places to practice. Specially designated areas and parks for skateboarders have worked in other communities with similar problems. If everyone would work together, it could work here.
Opinions, reasons, facts, and paragraphs will vary.

Page 29
8, 7, 2, 10, 1, 3, 5, 9, 6, 4
Paragraphs will vary.

Page 30
Directions will vary.

Page 31
Words and paragraphs will vary.

Page 32
Answers and book reviews will vary.

Page 33
Outlines and autobiographies will vary.

Page 34
Possible groupings:
Interesting Facts: one of the saltiest bodies of water in world, almost impossible for swimmers to sink in Dead Sea because of high density of salt
Dimensions: covers about 400 square miles, measures about 11 miles wide at widest point, measures about 31 miles long, bottom measures to depths of 2,622 feet below sea level
The Water in the Dead Sea: water comes from Jordan River and streams, water so salty that fish die immediately; nothing but simple microorganisms can survive in Dead Sea, water doesn't flow out of Dead Sea, water evaporates, leaving salt and other minerals behind

Page 35
Topic sentences and supporting sentences will vary.

Page 36
1. Spotting the doe in a clearing, I froze in my tracks and quietly took out my camera. I didn't want to startle the animal before getting at least one shot. Sensing my presence, the doe looked up at me. "Don't be frightened," I said in my most soothing voice. "I won't hurt you. I just want to take your picture."
2. After hiking for more than an hour up the steep trail, Jenny decided to take a break because her feet were killing her. Although she had worn her new hiking boots around the house all week, she soon realized that they were not sufficiently broken in. "I should have listened to Beth and worn my old boots," she grumbled to herself.
"Did you say something, Jenny?" Beth asked.

Page 37
Paragraphs in the first-person and third-person point of view will vary.

Page 38
Plans and story drafts will vary.

Page 39
It was Saturday morning, and Janelle was already in the kitchen.
"Breakfast will be ready in about five minutes!" Janelle yelled up to her brothers.
"Do you want some help?" offered Mom, who had just walked into the kitchen.
"Thanks, Mom," replied Janelle, "but I'd really like to do it myself."
"Okay," agreed Mom. "I'll just take the dog for a quick walk then."
Janelle popped the bread into the toaster and went back to the stove to check on the eggs and bacon. About a minute later, Ben said to Sam, "Do you smell something burning?"
"Yup," answered Sam. "It smells like burnt toast to me, and there goes the smoke alarm!"
"I guess Janelle's making breakfast again," laughed Ben, as they ran down to the kitchen.
"Do you want some help, Janelle?" Ben and Sam asked.

Page 40
Possible feelings:
1. angry
2. embarrassed
3. frightened
4. confident
5. surprised, happy
Dialogues will vary.

Page 41
Underlined words including the examples: whined, grumbled, promised, bellowed, admitted, whispered, assured, chuckled, insisted, muttered, countered, yelled, interrupted
Dialogues will vary.

Page 42
Paragraphs will vary.

Page 43
Sentences will vary.

Page 44
Phyllis the famous photographer, abruptly announced, bellowing yellow yak, everyone excitedly exclaimed, perfect piece of pie, obstinate tot named Otto, impudent imp implored, creepy crawly critter, whittled and whistled
Remaining answers will vary.

Page 45
Answers will vary.